1.800.799. SAFE (7233)

1.800.799. SAFE (7233)   ii

Is Your **Man**

Good for Your **Health**?

Unleash Your Inner Courage to Make

Positive Choices in Your Relationships

By Sunny Atkins

Disclaimer/Warning

This book is designed to give the reader ideas to better their lives. The information is derived from the author's personal experiences as best recollected. It is not the author's intention to provide medical or legal advice, professional diagnoses, and treatment or professional services to the reader.

This book provides general information for educational purposes only and is not a substitute for medical, legal or any professional advice. The author is not liable or responsible for any use of the information in this book in lieu of prompt consultation with a physician or other healthcare professional.

Published by

Aerostop Publishing

3481 Airport Road

Placerville, CA 95667

1.800.799. SAFE (7233)

iv

This book is dedicated to all women who find their every thought and move unwillingly controlled or violated by another human being.

While my stories are certainly not as extreme as it is for others it is my hope to reach others in similar situations. I want to show them that they are not alone and they too can find love in their lives and peace in their hearts.

Positive choices are the beginning. Live the life you want to live.

I also realize that relationships are more than a man and a woman. I also know women are not always the ones abused. However, this is what I know, so that is what I am writing about.

Acknowledgement

To everyone who had to deal with my seemingly endless journey to become a whole and healthy person. Thank you for your support and understanding.

Thank you to my wonderful husband of 20 years, Rick, for allowing and insisting that I be myself. You have taught me how to have a healthy equal and loving relationship. One filled with trust and tranquility.

To my wonderful daughters, Delia and Desiree. We have grown up together and, in many ways, you passed me by. You have been my guiding light and, many times, my reason for living. I taught you to be strong, confident and educated women. It was always my dream that your lives would be filled with love and that you would be kind and loving to others. You both are remarkable mothers. I thank you for my four beautiful grandchildren. Life goes on with healthy happy, safe families.

To the friends and family who were in my life as a child. Times were not easy for any of us. I cast no blame and I love you all.

To Caroline A. Wadlin MD, my friend, your constant flow of positive, self improvement books are paying off. Thank you for your belief in me and in the message. Without you this book would not have come to pass. I am truly grateful to you for you for all that you have taught me.

Thank you to Desiree, Delia, Lana, Kathy and Jeff for your hours of editing and making this book possible.

To the abuser in this story; I choose not to mention your name. I thought of calling you a beast or monster, but you are only a man who is mentally screwed up. I choose to not make you any bigger than you are. I do not want to glorify you in any way, so you are simply known as "he". I do, however, forgive you. I recognize my part of the relationship and that it takes two to tango.

Table of Contents

Chapter 1

A Few of Many Survival Stories

The Christmas Eve Blizzard of 1982 was considered the biggest storm in years, and even to this day is considered one of the biggest that Colorado has ever seen. Snowfall rates of 2 – 3 inches per hour were the norm during the day and winds screamed at 50mph, causing wind chill temperatures to plummet to as low as negative 35 degrees.

At around 11:00pm I huddled in an outside corner up at the school that is a block away from my house. Half dressed my head was bleeding, and I was feeling dizzy. I couldn't stop shaking from the cold and the fear. I worried, "Is he coming after me?" I was wearing clogs a pajama top and jeans. I had been changing for bed hoping he would settle down and leave me alone.

It began as a normal day in my life. The usual family stuff- breakfast, lunch and dinner. My kids were safe with their dad for the weekend. My current husband hadn't had a drink in a couple weeks and I had a slight calmness, and I began thinking things were going to be ok. We could get past New Year's Eve without an event. Then our neighbors invited us over for their New Year's Eve party. I became nervous.

The isolation and lack of interaction with other adults left me with a hunger for some social interaction, so I foolishly agreed to go to the party and My husband promised he wouldn't drink and that we would just stay for a little while. He went to the store for smokes. Then I noticed the brown bag he had in his hand as we walked into our neighbors. He had bought some alcohol. He looked at me and said

"Relax it'll be fine just wanted to bring a gift." I thought,

"Oh shit! This is not good!" He was bad enough when he drank beer, but he had just bought a 5th of something, I couldn't see what it was but, I knew it was hard liquor. He is violent when he drank that stuff. I thought.

"He is going to humiliate me in front of the neighbors; actually I'll be lucky if that's all. I'm really stuck so I'll try to gather my composure to be calm." The party was calm with around 10 people sitting around drinking and laughing. I tried to talk to others with one eye watching him as he started pouring the shots for others to drink. Of course it was one for them and one for him. He'd look over at me, raise his glass towards me and say

"Hey Doll here's to you"

"Fuck, I'm in trouble" I thought. How the hell am I going to get him out of here? And when I do what's going to happen?" The knot in my stomach turned a little tighter.

"Don't be such a tight ass, here have a little drink" he continued. I took it thinking

"I'm going to need it."

I take the glass hoping to slow him down, but he only found another one.

"We should leave" I suggested

"What the fuck for? We just got here!"

Within the hour he was drunk. He started telling some guy what a bad housekeeper I was; Of course everyone could hear what he was saying. I was humiliated and not sure how I was going to get him out of there. Somehow I did; but not without everyone there being upset and scared for me. They could see I was afraid, and that he was volatile. It didn't stop when we got home. I knew it wouldn't, but was praying he would pass out.

We walked home two doors down, and then it began. He accused me;

"I saw you look at the guy in the blue shirt."

"What guy?" I asked. I wasn't looking at anyone besides my husband as he humiliated me and got hammered. I explained that someone asked me if I wanted a drink and that I said no thank you. Otherwise I sat talking to no one. Then the verbal abuse continued,

"You're so stupid. You can't even go to a party and have a good time without bitching at me".

I clarified that "he was the one saying rude things about me and that he was very loud and obnoxious. "

I tried to change the subject by getting ready for bed, hoping and praying to be left alone. As I was changing into pajamas he escalated from verbal abuse to physical abuse. He pushed me into the wall and I hit my head on the corner of a shelf. My head was bleeding, and I distinctly remember him saying with red devil eyes

"Where's your God now?"

From somewhere deep within me came a strength I'd never felt before.

I yelled "Right Here!" I pushed him in the chest and he flew 20 feet backwards. I was able to run out the door with him yelling,

"Yeah, you better run you stupid bitch, I hope you fuckin' die!" with a laugh that chilled me to the bone. I ran out into the frigid temperatures barely dressed. I ran for my life.

"Is he following me? Where should I go?" Crying uncontrollably and shaking from the fear and cold, my face was blotchy red from crying and I could not catch my breath.

"I have to calm down, I have to hide until he passes out, then I can go home."

"I'm so stupid! Why did I agree to go to the party? It's my fault. I really thought we could have a good time."

"We can never have a good time it's always dramatic".

"I hate him,"

"I hate him,"

"I have to leave him… yeah, sure… and go where?"

It was dark, cold, and my clothes were soaking wet. With it still snowing and my head hurting, I knew that I needed to stay awake with the head trauma.

I would surely die from hyperthermia. I sat in the freezing cold trying not to pass out. Shaking uncontrollably, I was afraid to go to the neighbors because that bastard might go there and cause trouble for them. I was embarrassed to show my face to anyone. But I knew I couldn't stay out here and freeze to death. My girls needed me. I needed them.

So after about 45 minutes I circled around through snow into the alley to see if I could tell if he was passed out or not. The door was wide open and lights were on. It looked like he was watching TV. I didn't dare go back. My mind was racing. Where should I go? I had no friends, he made sure of that. My family lived in another state and I'd never want to admit I was so weak and stupid to get myself into a

SAFE (7233)

7

situation like this. I believed that he was really a good person, it's just when he drank he was horrible. I couldn't go to his family; they were afraid of him as well. I couldn't go to the police; because he didn't really hit me, he only pushed me. I shouldn't have talked back to him. I should've just said "I'm sorry. Yeah you're right. I am stupid," instead of arguing.

Who would pay to get him out of jail? I didn't have any money. If I left him there, the next time he'll kill me for sure. Besides the roads were bad and it was very late. I didn't want to bother anyone.

Out of desperation I finally decided to go the neighbors and begged their forgiveness. Everyone had left and they were just cleaning up. My neighbor insisted I come in and stay there with them. They fed me and gave me a warm place to sleep. I was very grateful and very embarrassed.

The next morning I went home to the door wide open and all the lights on. He was passed out on the couch. When he woke up he was sorry. He apologized for yelling at me and said,

"I was just jealous of that guy talking to you." He continued to say,

"I was so worried about you, why did you leave?

"I love you so much; I'd die if anything ever happened to you. "Let's do something fun today."

(It's called the Honeymoon phase. The severity of the event will determine the length of the honeymoon phase. This one was good for about 3 weeks.)

This kind of thing went on for seven years. It happened on the average of about once a week. Sometimes it could stretch to two weeks. I kept a small bag packed and hidden by the back door for my girls in case we had to leave in a hurry.

I fought back!

Before I was laid off, I would walk about six blocks at about five thirty in the morning to catch a bus to take me across town. I didn't mind, really. It was my time to myself, except for the times when homeless people or other strange characters would try to engage or harass me. Because of the rain and snowy weather, there were times when I would be soaked when I got to work or back home again. I enjoyed the exercise, even though it was often dark out. I would walk down the middle of the street because I was nervous about what could have been lurking in the bushes. I guess I watched too much TV. I was once told that I was conceited, to think that someone was always trying to get me.

After I was laid off money was very scarce and of course he wasn't working. We were relying on my unemployment and child support. Every time the phone rang, I'd cringe, because bill collectors called constantly and some were not very nice. For heat I would roll up newspapers really tight so they would burn slowly in our wood stove. It didn't work very well, but it kept me busy. Our oven didn't work so I had to make everything in the microwave oven. Cookies were interesting.

I don't remember how it started or what it was about. It was in the middle of the day and my girls were in school. There was no alcohol involved this time that I distinctly remember. Suddenly, he was yelling at me and pushing me. I remember thinking,

"I'm not taking this shit anymore",
And I pushed him back. My attempt to fight back left me lying on the floor unconscious. When I regained consciousness he was kicking me in the stomach, yelling

"Go ahead and die bitch, it would be just like you to mess up my life even more!"
He saw that I was alive and left the house. How considerate of him to make sure I was alive. I crawled to the living room and onto the couch and cried for hours. My head was pounding and I was nauseous, I was very dizzy. I willed myself to stay awake because

my girls would be home soon and I could not let them see me like this. I knew if I fell asleep I might not wake up. My babies needed me. I had to be strong.

I had a routine doctor's appointment a few days later and I told him I had fallen to explain the bruises. I was looking into getting a reversal to my tubal. Yes, I thought if I had his baby he'd be nicer to me. That's how screwed up I was. The Doctor was so nice to me. He suggested that maybe it wasn't a good idea. It was obvious that we had no money and I think he could see I was being abused. Luckily, I decided he was right. It was such a treat for a man to be so caring to me. This was foreign to me my whole life. It gave me hope that there were other men out there who would treat me better. Perhaps I wasn't as useless as he always told me I was.

A Mini Trip Turned Ugly

For some reason, there was extra money. I can't remember from what. We decided to have a mini vacation, so we headed to Aspen for an overnight stay. We packed up the girls, who were two and five years old, and we were off for a seemingly pleasant family trip. We found an inexpensive motel with a pool. To a stranger, we appeared to be your average family with children swimming and laughing. Then he got mad at me because I wouldn't have sex with him in the pool with 6 or 7 other people and my children only a few feet away. So it began again, I knew this wasn't going to be a good time at all. Later, we found some take out burgers instead of the nice dinner we were promised. Back at our room as we ate our dinner he showered and changed, applying after shave. The knots in my stomach tightened. I can still recall the smell of his pungent after shave. He departed at around 6:00, to get some smokes, of course.

"I'll be right back." I knew different.

At around midnight he still wasn't back. I lay waiting, worrying what would happen? Would he get in the car and drive drunk? I actually hoped he would and that he would die. Or would he get thrown in jail and I'd have to get him out? Would he leave us all there? Or would he come back and hurt us? He staggered in around 2:15, the bars obviously having closed. He proceeded to pass out on our bed and then vomited all over me. I was grateful he was out. As I cleaned myself up, I looked at him. My thoughts were,

"You disgusting pig!" The next day it was as if nothing happened, as usual.

Jesus

It wasn't always about me, and there wasn't always alcohol involved. This one particular time, it was his sister who he chose to impress his rage on. He decided he didn't like it that she was living with a guy and not married; even though it was ok that we had done that. Go figure. We needed to go to her house to pick up my girls. When we arrived they were having a barbeque. He walked over to the table and picked up a 6" knife and grabbed his sister, holding the knife to her throat. I jumped on his back trying to stop him. Fortunately she had been able to get her hand between her throat and the knife. Everyone was screaming, yelling and crying. She screamed "Jesus!", and the knife broke. It all happened so fast, from beginning to end was about 5 minutes. Everyone was very upset, but he wouldn't leave. They were saying,

"Sunny, stay here." He said,

"SHE goes with me!"

I knew I'd better go in order to get him away from them, he wasn't mad at me at the time so I prayed it would be ok. Generally, he was calmer when the kids were around. My two and half year old walked over to him took his hand and said, "Lets go, Daddy." He followed her like a little puppy.

Of course I was scared, I was always scared. I was cautious, doing my best to not upset him in anyway. We went home and had dinner, again, as if nothing had happened.

You are probably wondering why the police weren't called. Everyone knew if they were called, all of us were in even more danger than before. We were certain he would get out and we would all pay for it then.

Lying to the Police

One night he had been out drinking, and of course, driving. He sideswiped a car and fled the scene. When he got home he told me to say I was the one driving the car. In case the police were going to come, because the car was registered to me.

"What? Are you kidding me? I can't say I was driving." I was sick to my stomach at the thought of lying to the police. The next day his mother told me

"You have to say it was you, so my son doesn't go to jail."

"They won't do anything to you, you have a clean record." I was furious with all of them for having no regard for me at all. I was their pasty. They didn't care about me; they just wanted to use me.

That night around ten o'clock, there was a knock at the door. He ran to the back room and listened. It was the police. I welcomed them in, I was shaking. They said a witness saw a man with dark hair flee the scene of an accident. The car was mine. Since the beat up car was in the driveway they see that my car has been in an accident, and asked me to explain. I told them that it was me and I was sorry. They explained "that a witness said it was a dark haired man with stubble." I said

"My husband and I had been arguing and I was upset. I had makeup on my face and it had been raining, I had a scarf on covering my hair."

They saw him hovering in the back room and decided to play along. I am sure they knew the truth that he was intimidating me into lying to them. I had to Go to court and plead guilty to a misdemeanor hit and run that I didn't commit. I was humiliated; I had never even been in a court room before. He waited outside for me. I was scared to death. We had to borrow money from a friend to pay the fine. They actually thought I had done this horrible thing. His family laughed later at how we cheated the police.

Chapter 2

Grace

A Small Gesture of Reaching Out

A woman came into my life; It was such a long time ago that I can't remember her name. So, I am going to call her Grace, because her generosity changed my life forever. It could only be by the Grace of God that she was sent to me.

I remember her having a beautiful face and short, stylishly cut gray hair. I didn't have any friends, so I believe God slipped her in under the radar to befriend me. The time we spent together was extremely short. In the 2 months I knew her we probably only spent an hour alone talking. Grace took the initiative and gave me a book, Wayne Dyer's <u>The Erroneous Zones</u>. I remember thinking I hadn't read a book since high school, other than college texts for accounting.

When she gave me the book she said

"This is a really good book that I have read and you might enjoy it. No it's not about sex [because of the title]."

So I began reading it. The response I received from him was:

"What are you doing?"

"Where the hell did you get that stupid book?"

With a very suspicious eye, he watched me

read. When I mentioned that Grace gave me this book, he manipulated me not to see her again. He did not want me learning and getting any of my own ideas.

The funny thing is, the more I read, the dumber he looked, and the smarter I felt. I learned that the words he used to tear me down were a reflection on him and not me. If I didn't accept his words as my thoughts and turned my thoughts into actions I could see the world and myself in a whole new light. I honestly believe this book saved my life. Of course, it was a tool that God used through the writer and then through Grace. For all of this I am eternally grateful.

I wondered what it was that Grace saw when she looked at me. If I recollect my appearance and my behavior at that stage of my life it would be something like this. I was thin (that was the only good part, except everyone says I was too thin)- my 5'8" large boned frame was only carrying 115 pounds. I was constantly nervous, very jumpy, very introverted, never looking anyone in the eye, and I had a negative attitude. If we were around other people I didn't talk because he convinced me that:

"No one cares what you have to say."

While I never went without makeup or my hair un-styled, it didn't cover up the dark circles or the despair in my eyes. I thought I was fat and plain looking. After all, that's what I was told.

I was also told:

"No one else loves you,"

"Especially not your father. He didn't even want you when you were born! Why else didn't you meet him until you were 13 years old?"

What kept me going day after day? My children did. I love my girls more than anything and I was a good mother, but not a great mother. How could I be? I was in survival mode. I thought I was doing everything that I could to protect them. Fortunately they had their father to go spend weekends with. They were safe with their dad and so they were not always subjected to the weekly cruelty inflicted upon their mother, by their stepfather.

In my mind I believed that since he didn't hurt them they weren't being affected. I later found that wasn't the case. They listened to their mother being verbally abused on a daily basis, called every name in the book and seeing dinner thrown on the ground because it had become cold. I had zero self esteem, zero confidence and poor communication skills. I couldn't carry on a conversation about current events or anything about myself. My point of view was censored; and I had no existence. I can remember being at a job interview, and they asked me to tell them something about myself. I talked about my husband. At that moment I realized I had drowned.

"Sunny" really didn't exist anymore. My thoughts were my own, so I kept them to myself, inside my head where they were safe. If I let them out they would be destroyed and so would I; even more than I already was. I dreamt of a life where I could share my thoughts and feelings with another human being without ridicule, or worse. The reason the book I was given was so pivotal to me was because Dr. Dyer said we have choices. Now, this seems like a simple thing to most of you, because of course we have choices and we are responsible for our choices. I did not know this. I believe I am not alone. We are told what to do all of our lives, so we just take whatever is given us without much thought about it.

I also learned I am in control of my thoughts. Just because someone says I am stupid. I have to realize,… no, it's not me that's stupid. I would never tell another human being such a horrible thing. I choose not to accept your words as my own thoughts or beliefs. So thank you Grace and thank you Dr. Wayne Dyer.

Chapter 3

How did I get here?

A Glimpse into My Childhood

When I was six my stepfather adopted me. I was told that my real father did not want to meet me. In fact, I didn't even meet him until I was 13 years old. Come to find out my father paid my step father $500 to adopt me. At the time he clearly did not want to be a father to me.

Despite the fact that my biological father didn't want me. I grew up in an abusive environment. My stepfather had short man's complex and a quick temper. That combination and a sick need to show his power and control over myself and six siblings. He worked in construction, so work was inconsistent and we moved every year. Every year I started a new school and had to make new friends, which was torture for me. The tension in our *home* was always so thick you could cut it with a knife. On a regular basis, I remember holding my stomach, rocking back and forth and crying. In the next room my brothers were being drug out of bed by their father, and kicked in the stomach, for not picking up their toys or something stupid. Once he washed a load of laundry and forgot to add laundry soap.

I said "Wow that was stupid!" He slapped me across the face. I think I was about 8 years old.

If any of us did anything wrong he would hide the belt and then tell us we had 5 minutes to find it or else we were going to get beat worse. I can distinctly remember one of my brothers, who was about 11 at the time, crying and pleading,

"Where is the belt, I have to find it." He was in such a hurry to find the belt, but that just meant he was going to get his ass beat anyway. Another form of discipline that was administered was having us stand while facing the wall in a corner for several hours. We had to have our hands behind our back and could not touch the wall. He would even punish/humiliate us even when we had company over.

He was sick and loved to torture us. I really hated **hate** this man. Of course we had chores, who didn't? However, we were his slaves. After washing the dishes for a family of 8, he found one spoon that I failed to wash and dry. He decided to teach me a lesson, at six years old, not to be so negligent. He yelled at me as he pulled out every dish, pan, glass, and piece of silverware and made me wash and dry it again. I could barely reach into the bottom of the very deep stainless steel sink. I can remember crying while all of my clothes were soaking wet as I continued to wash all the dishes again. Plus it was late and I school the next day. All I wanted to do was go to bed. I can remember my mom trying to help by sneaking dishes back into the cabinet. She knew what he was doing was not right, but she could not stand up to him either.

She was heavily influenced by him not to think for herself.

I too, was taught *not* to think for myself. Throughout childhood and adolescence he told me,

"You are not smart enough to cross the road without asking someone first."

How is that for building the self esteem of a young girl? While I understand that children should not cross the road by themselves; it was the language he used to "teach" me that was so degrading.

My self esteem was so bad that I can remember being late for class as a third grader and scared to death of walking in alone. The thought of having everyone look at me made me sick to my stomach. So I decided to hide in the bathroom all day to avoid the humiliation.

Yet I was responsible for taking care of my 4 brothers for hours on end at the age of 10 while my mom worked endless hours as a cook, or cleaning houses.

Because I could not think for myself, at one point in my teens I found myself thinking that if someone were drowning, I would have to ask if I should help them. I was so used to being told what to think. That thought woke me up from a programmed state. But I had no tools or skills for self confidence. I had no self esteem at all. I was starved for someone to validate that I was good at anything or worth anything.

I was told girls are just supposed to get married and have babies. There was no reason to learn anything. I desperately wanted more for myself and I often wondered how could I become a better person without any support? Someone must think I am worth more. Someone must think I am smart and maybe even pretty. I searched for attention and affection in all the wrong places. This mentality as a teenager can be tragic. I had a few boyfriends; I mostly liked the hippie type for some reason. Of course my parents didn't like any of them; until I brought home a clean cut young man fresh out of the military. This boy said "Yes, ma'am" and "Thank you sir." They thought he was perfect. Little did they know that the minute the door was closed he was all over me. Their judgment quickly lost credibility.

Because I *was* a natural follower, I experimented with hallucinogenic drugs as a teen to find a place in the world. Luckily, I did not get completely lost in drugs, because the out of control sensation was not worth it and not my thing. There was also a nagging paranoia that my parents would find out I was not where I was supposed to be. I was constantly in fear of my step father. It wasn't all bad. I remember the great relief of the tension at our house when my cousins would come over and we'd all pile in the back of a truck with our inner tubes, (we didn't have air mattresses) and head to the lake. We'd play in the sun and water for hours on end. We are lucky to be alive after riding in the back of trucks, in the sun, with no sun screen. We even drank out of hoses. All big no-no's today. My childhood wasn't all bad.

Chapter 4

The Cycle Continues

As an Adult

I was determined not to continue the vicious cycle of abuse, but I was fixated on being accepted and as a result I found myself in an abusive marriage. We met at work. He was attractive, charming and paid attention to me. What more could I ask for? Well, he was also dangerous and somehow I found that exciting. Who doesn't love a bad boy? He had previously been a heroin addict and had told me stories of robbing 7-elevens. I overlooked that he lived with his mother at the age of 30. What the hell was I thinking?

I will put my mindset into words.

- I needed to be needed,
- He appeared to be well liked
- He appeared to be worldly and exciting
- He said I was cute (what a sucker I was)
- I was the only person who understood him

Why in the world I thought I could make him a better person is beyond me now.

Well that kind of thinking really backfired. I turned into a pathetic, do anything, needy person. With low self esteem to begin with, it was an easy trap for me to fall into. This weakness only fuels the fire for an abusive relationship.

After working long hours into the night together he would take me to Five Points (known as The Harlem of the West), where I did not feel safe. He needed to get his booze and it was after hours. So, he took me to a bootlegger establishment with dirty couches filled with passed out drunks. The eyes of the patrons who were not passed out lingered over me. I felt very naked and violated by their stares. The lone swinging 40 watt light bulb burns in my memory. The lighting was ominous and I should have known then that this guy did not have my best interests in mind.

Early in our relationship he was in a car accident with my ex-brother in law. We all worked at the same place, and one day they rode to work together. Because of the accident, he lost partial use of his right arm, so he could not work. In my way of thinking, if he had not met me, he would have never been in that car and the accident might not have happened. So, it was my fault. The guilt of that delusion made me feel that I had to take care of him. The next thing I knew we were married, and the burden was contractually mine.

His inability to use his dominant arm made him a really angry drunk. He could not work and had to go to physical therapy. He felt like half a man without use of his arm and this seriously threatened his machismo. He had a lot of time to conjure up exaggerations of reality. It was small and stupid things that would set him off. One time I wore shoes to church that made me taller than him. His insecurity caused him to lash out verbally and physically at me when we got home. I threw those shoes away.

I constantly worried about how I could make him happy and meet his needs. I sacrificed my own identity. I allowed myself to be isolated from having any friends, because I was so consumed with keeping him from becoming agitated. I had no family in the area. It was his mother that said he hit me because I didn't pray enough. She said that I was the strength of the family and the burden was mine. His family was aware that I recognized my duty of keeping him calm, which made their lives better. This meant that he would not bother them as much. Yes, more stress, more guilt, and of course, something else I didn't do right or enough of. His mother was a hypocrite who would go to church, and then curse at the drivers in the parking lot for not moving fast enough. I could not understand how someone could attend church services and then moments later slander everyone from the minister to the guy in the parking lot who was taking too long. This was the support system I was stuck with.

I remember thinking that if I loved him enough he would change. This thinking only made it worse because I had become a doormat. Looking back, love had nothing to do with changing him. In his eyes, I was pathetic. It wasn't until I finally stood up to him that he gained any respect for me. However, in my experience, it was not a good idea to stand up for myself during a fight, especially when he was drinking, because this led to severe abuse. I thought I had some kind of power that would make him change, and I had a compulsion to nurture and feel needed. This state of mind, in addition to constantly being told I was stupid and worthless, made me feel I had no other options.

One evening I was watching The Burning Bed with Farrah Fawcett. If you haven't seen it, Farrah is in an abusive relationship and retaliates by tying her sleeping husband to the bed and lighting it on fire. I don't condone this act of revenge, but it was liberating to watch. He came home to me watching this move and I loved the feeling of fear that I saw in him as I glanced his way with a vengeful smile. I also felt a little power in that moment. He was nicer for a longer period of time.

I later learned and educated my daughters that we don't have the right to ask someone to change. If you don't like that they smoke or drink and how they treat you, then move on. We can only hope to change their hair and clothes. But that's not 100%.

Chapter 5

The Final Escape

All I had to give me hope was the book from Grace. As I read the book, and talked more to God, the stronger I felt. The true test was another fight, when he threw every piece of clothing I owned onto the living room floor. The next morning I wasn't affected by the honeymoon phase. He said he was sorry, I said "sure you are." I felt strong: I didn't make eye contact with him and ignored him. It made him crazy. I began packing boxes and stashing them in closets.

I had called my grandmother and asked to borrow some money. I explained I needed to get away and didn't have any means to become safe. She immediately mailed me $500.00. When I received the check that my wonderful grandfather had filled out with his scratchy 80 year old handwriting, I noticed he forgot to sign the check. I almost lost it at that moment, because the day had come when I had planned to go rent a truck and pack it up and leave. I chose this day because he was supposed to be away for a business meeting.

A little voice inside me said he meant to sign it; he would be upset if I was hurt because he forgot to sign it. So I signed it myself. God forgive me, I was so nervous, I cashed the check and got a ride from a neighbor to the truck rental. I backed into our house and started frantically loading it.

Suddenly he appeared home early. My neighbor lady must have called him.

He said, "What do you think you are doing?" and I said "I'm leaving you, what's it look like."

He proceeded to follow me from room to room begging me not to leave. Telling me I can't take this and I can't take that.

I yelled "What the hell are you talking about? I bought it."

He said "If you want to enjoy it then you have to do it here."

God was really with me that day because I wasn't affected at all by his attempt to break me down. He tried being angry and intimidating and that didn't work so he moved on to begging and pleading. It made it so easy to leave, because I saw how pathetic he really was.

The only furniture he let me take was my girls' bedroom furniture. I didn't care, it was only stuff. I just wanted out of there. Then he spoke to his business partner who told him to get me to sign divorce papers before I left. He called his partner's attorney and asked them to draw up divorce papers today! I joyfully agreed to divorce him immediately and rode with him to the attorney's office to sign them. Hallelujah!

We arrived at the attorney's office and I wasn't going to do any waiting, I told him they'd better be ready. There were several other people in the office. I was reading the divorce papers and everything looked ok, until I got to the part that said he wanted joint custody of <u>my</u> daughters. I came unglued and turned into a huge bitch and went off on him and everyone in the room.

"What's this? What do you mean joint custody? My volume escalated,

"What do you mean joint custody? They aren't even your children and I wouldn't let you within 10 feet of them"

By now I was yelling and I was shaking in the middle of a waiting room at an attorney's office,

"Get this out of here right now!, How dare you! You think you can abuse me for seven years and I'm going to let you have anything to do with my children? Are you fucking crazy?"

He kept saying

"Calm down, calm down, they'll take it out, calm down. I love them, and I just wanted to be able to see them."

"Then I guess you should have fuckin treated me better, shouldn't you?" The attorney crossed the section out, and I signed.

We went back to the house, where I continued to load the truck. I was almost done when my girls came home from school. I sent them back to get anything they had left at school because we were leaving. They hurried to the school and retrieved their things. My plan was to go to Grace's for the night and then head to California in the morning. I didn't let him know any of this.

He cried to the girls and told them how much he loved them and that made them cry. Even with his sob story they were so relieved to be getting away from him. We jumped into the truck and headed to Grace's house.

The next morning we headed toward California. I had some little cereal boxes that the girls were eating as we pulled into a weigh station hours outside of Denver. Usually, they wave you on but for some reason I was told to stop. I stopped and a police officer walked out very cautiously with his hand on his gun because he was ready to draw it on me. My mind raced about what was going to happen,

"Oh my God! They know I signed that check!" When he got to the truck he asked for my driver's license. He was concerned about the truck and didn't ask me about any check forgery. Evidently someone fitting my description had just stolen a truck like the one I was driving. He saw the girls and realized I'm not the criminal they were looking for. Even though I felt like one, because of the check. That's how naïve I was. It would take weeks before the check would be discovered, if ever at all.

Then we were pulled over in the middle of Utah at a road block. The officer there told me I was lucky my children looked like me, because they set up road blocks without warning and search vehicles looking for missing children out there in the middle of nowhere.

Next we got stuck in Nevada. I was driving a U-Haul truck and we needed chains to get over the pass. I decided to rent a hotel room in Carson City, even though I was running out of money. The girls thought it was fun. Then next day we drove to Truckee to see how far we could get. I was thinking highway 80 was a better road and possibly safer. My hope was that we could get over the pass without chains, because I sure didn't have the extra money to buy chains for the UHaul truck. When we arrived we found out that they would not let anyone over the pass without chains. As you can imagine, I was beside myself because I only had enough money to either buy chains or feed my children. I pulled into yet another area where they sell chains and a very nice man came up and told me it would cost $100.00. I just broke down and started crying uncontrollably. Poor guy, he was so nice, he gave me chains and installed them. He made me promise to give them to someone else who needed them. His generosity and kindness saved our lives that night. While driving I was very happy to have the chains on as we crept over the snow covered pass. The visibility was very low, and cars were sliding all over the place. It was a terrifying 20 miles that took a couple of hours; I was spent and emotionally drained.

I arrived at my aunts and was ready to sleep for about a week. As I was pulling into her driveway I began feeling hopeful for the new life ahead of me. My life was now up to me and will not be driven by someone else. I will do everything possible to empower my daughters to make themselves a priority, always.

Someone once said to me as a joke **"It's Mind over matter, I don't mind and you don't matter"**. I care very much for the person who said this and he meant no harm, but if you talk to any person who has been abused it's likely a lingering feeling they always have. These words cut me like a knife, and it's been over 20 years since I have been in an abusive relationship.

I do matter, and so do you!

Chapter 6

Ownership of Your Role

in an Abusive Relationship!

What is your role in your relationship? Yes, you have a part, whether you like to admit it or not. It's time to own it. You have allowed yourself be verbally and/or physically abused. I know these are harsh words. The first time I heard them I was devastated, but then I started thinking about it, and it's true. However, my friend we all have choices. It's time to assess the choices you have made and realize the better ones you could have made. Now is the time to make new, healthier choices. Start now!

As a child you were trapped and had no power. So anything that happened to you as a child, it's time to let it go. I know some things are unbearable and you feel it's impossible to let it go. Ask yourself, what good is it doing me today? Is it healthy for me to dwell on it? Probably not. Get professional help, if at all possible.

Look in the mirror and look deep for that strong person hiding behind the face that is full of pain. Talk to her and tell her she is pretty; she is smart; she is loveable. Take a deep breath and make a commitment to yourself to become a happier, healthier person. You are the only one who can do this for yourself. Practice this every day, even a couple times a day, until you believe it; Practice it until you realize you are a good person who deserves to be happy. It's a new day, a new you, a stronger you. No one has the right to treat you in a way *you don't want* them to.

There are many degrees of abuse. Make sure you aren't causing the abuse by behaving inappropriately yourself.

Here are some things to be sure you are not doing.

Are you a drama queen? Are you laying some drama on him the minute he walks in the door?

Do you sit around with your friends male bashing? If he is not a good man, then move on. But if he is a good guy, then the negative energy that comes from female-male bashing can cause a volatile situation.

Do you make fun of or speak poorly about your man? Again, this is not healthy. Perhaps you need to rethink your reason for being with him. No one deserves to be belittled.

Do you nag your mate about everything? Pick your battles. Does he work all day and then leave his socks on the floor? Pick them up or leave them there. He'll get the hint. If you just can't stand it, have a calm, rational conversation about it with him. Say it once and drop it.

Do you call him names? This is never a good idea. Do you argue when he is drinking? That's a dangerous thing to do and a time to keep your mouth shut. Discuss your opinion when he's not intoxicated.

Chapter 7

Are You Ready to Leave...Really?

It's Time to Change how you think!

What happens the day after a fight or abusive confrontation? How do you feel? Is your partner sorry? Does he promise it will never happen again? This is known as the honeymoon phase.

Does he agree to counseling, agree to attend meetings at Alcoholics Anonymous, or take Antabuse[1]? Did he buy you a present? Does it feel better? If yes, then you are not ready to leave. Do you find yourself thinking?

"He's really a good person, he's just misunderstood, I understand him and no one else does. He needs me." Some women say,

"When it hurts too much, I will leave," but not until you finally feel numb to the day after honeymoon phase with the groveling- **then you are ready**. In this case, the *groveling* does not make up for the harm done. The empowerment begins when you stop feeling sorry for him and start thinking of your own survival, and that of your children. **You are ready to leave** when the guilt gifts and the words,

"I'm sorry, please forgive me. I love you. I need you," don't melt your heart into a puddle of pity and self hatred.

---

[1] Antabuse is a drug that deters use of alcohol. The drug blocks the breakdown of alcohol, thus causing unpleasant side effects (e.g., vomiting, upset stomach).

When you are ready you will feel strong, disgusted by him and his excuses. And above all **you are ready to leave when**; you stop making it your fault. *Only then, my friend, is when you are ready to leave an abusive relationship and stay away and not **until then**.*

Chapter 8

Your Support System

Often people in abusive relationships find themselves without a support structure. If you are in an abusive relationship and you have maintained friends and family, then consider yourself lucky. It is much easier to leave if there are people who can help you pick up the pieces afterward. However, family will recognize the abuse in your relationship and feel uncomfortable around the abuser. They are likely to feel helpless in your fight to survive. Perhaps you made choices that your friends and family didn't agree with. If you are anything like me, then, you probably wouldn't have listened to advice from family or friends, anyway.

There are two perspectives to consider; yours and theirs. You likely feel like others would not understand your situation and they would just be judgmental. After all, you still see some good in this person who abuses you.

The perspective of your friends and family might be that they don't want to get hurt; they don't agree with your choices; or they cannot financially support you. They may fear that if they go in and help you, then he may threaten them or hurt you more.

Perhaps you have used drugs or alcohol and you need help getting clean and sober. Your friends and family may not know how to handle your habits. Tackle one problem at a time. Ask friends and family for support in attending a rehabilitation program. Can they help you with a drug or alcohol problem? Can they take care of your children while you are getting the help you need?

Once your family and friends see your commitment to self–improvement, chances are, they will be more motivated to help you with your journey.

Get away from the source of the problem first. If others help you, who's to say you won't go back to the abusive relationship. Go back to chapter 7 and really think about "*Are* you ready to leave….Really?"

If they help you, will he come around and threaten everyone they love? People watch TV, they see what happens and it's scary.

Because your friends and family watch TV, or because of past issues with you, can they trust you?

I know these are harsh words. For some of you it doesn't apply. But if just one of you reads this and says,

"Oh yeah, I've been kind of nasty to my family. I better get my act together!" then it's worth it.

Chapter 9

Is There A Problem?

**First we need to
acknowledge that there
is a problem!**

Do you live in fear?

Do you think you

deserve your life?

How to know if you are in an abusive relationship?

- Have you ever been told that you are stupid and that no one loves you, except him of course?
- Have you ever been told that you are not one of the pretty people?
- Do you get a knot in your stomach when you are running late and the house isn't "just so?" Or the dinner is not ready when he gets home?
- Do you find yourself agreeing with everything he says, and you then ask yourself later "do I really believe that"?
- Do you constantly shush the kids to be quiet so they don't disturb him?
- Do you hold your breath when he gets home? Checking his mood, knowing the evening will hinge on it?
- Does he make regular verbal and physical threats? Does he tell you that you are worthless and unattractive?
- Have you ever lied to someone about an injury that was inflicted upon you by being pushed or hit?

- Have you lied about not attending an event because he was angry about something?
  - Have you ever been accused of having an affair just because you said hi to a coworker or classmate?
  - Have you been accused of having an affair because you smiled at a person of the opposite sex on the street as they walked by?

Does the person you love...

- Constantly keep track of your time?
- Act jealous and possessive?
- Accuse you of being unfaithful or flirting?
- Discourage relationships with your friends and family?
- Prevent or discourage you from working, interacting with friends or attending school?
- Constantly criticize or belittle you?
- Control all finances and force you to account for what you spend? (Reasonable, cooperative budgeting accepted.)

- Humiliate you in front of others?
  (Making "jokes" at your expense.)
- Destroy or take your personal property or sentimental items?
- Have affairs?
- Threaten to hurt you, your children or pets? Threaten to use a weapon?
- Push, hit, slap, punch, kick, or bite you or your children?
- Force you to have sex against your will, or demand sexual acts you are uncomfortable with?

What Is Abuse?

Abuse can be physical, emotional, sexual, or verbal. It is often a combination.

Everyone has heard the songs about how much love can hurt. That doesn't mean physical harm. Someone who loves you should never abuse you. Healthy relationships involve respect, trust, and consideration for the other person.

Sadly, many relationships turn abusive. Abuse can sometimes be mistaken for intense feelings of caring or concern. It can even seem flattering. Think of a friend whose boyfriend or girlfriend is insanely jealous. Maybe it seems like your friend's partner really cares about him or her. But actually, excessive jealousy and controlling behavior are not signs of affection at all. Love involves respect and trust; it doesn't mean constantly worrying about the possible end of the relationship.

Abuse can be physical, emotional, or sexual. Slapping, hitting, and kicking are forms of physical abuse that can occur in both romances and friendships.

Emotional abuse (such as teasing, bullying, and humiliating others) can be difficult to recognize because it doesn't leave any visible scars. Threats, intimidation, putdowns, and betrayal are all harmful forms of emotional abuse that can really hurt — not just during the time it's happening, but long after too.

Sexual abuse can happen to anyone, man or woman. It's never right to be forced into any type of sexual experience that you don't want.

The first step in getting out of an abusive relationship is to realize that you have the right to be treated with respect and not be physically or emotionally harmed by another person.

Chapter 10

Is my Friend Being Abused?

How can I tell?

Have you ever said to yourself,

"If it's so horrible, why doesn't she just leave?" I'm here to tell you that physical abuse is bad and you can die from it. However, bruises heal with time. It's the scaring that comes with verbal and emotional abuse that has the lasting effect. When you are told over and over again that no one wants you except him, and that you are plain or ugly or stupid, you come to accept that as the truth. Are you being isolated, so that you aren't able to have a friend to share with? He'll isolate you because otherwise, your friend might convince you to leave him (your abusive partner). In her mind he is the only one who loves her.

There is a behavior that is detectable, even in the best actresses. Often a person won't be able to carry on a conversation and look you straight in the eye. Do you see her instantly stiffen when their significant other walks through the door? Does she become nervous and anxious to please him? You can actually see her energy change just at the sound of his voice. The somewhat confident person you were just speaking to, turns into a battered puppy, practically cowering in the corner, right before your eyes.

Some Things to Look For

- Are there unexplained bruises, broken bones, sprains, or marks on them?
- Excessive guilt or shame for no apparent reason.
- Withdrawing from friends and family.
- Avoiding social events with excuses that don't seem to make any sense.

It takes a lot of courage to admit being abused. Let your friend know that you are offering your full support. Let them know that they did not "ask for it" and that they deserve to be treated better. A person who is being abused needs someone to listen without judgment. They need your patience and love. Your friend also needs your encouragement to get help immediately.

You may not understand, but try to let them think that you do. It's ok to suggest *gently* that they leave. However, if she isn't ready, it will destroy your relationship with the abused person. She may even tell the abuser what you've suggested. Remember she still has moments when she thinks she is happy. Then you won't be able to keep an eye on her at all.

Abused people usually feel like it's their fault or that they don't deserve any better. But abuse is never deserved. Help your friend understand that it is not his or her fault. Your friend is not a bad person. Be sure you don't say anything offensive about the abuser. Again gently, suggest they get professional help.

Domestic violence is <u>no longer</u> a taboo topic that cannot be discussed about in polite society. It is still difficult for the one abused.

Most are embarrassed, afraid and have lost complete control of their self worth and self confidence. Be patient, supportive and nonjudgmental.

Chapter 11

How to Escape

Tips for a Quick Escape

If you have no money or you don't have access to a checking account because he sees everything that comes and goes, then it's time to find other resources. Do you have a budget for the grocery store? When shopping get small amounts of cash back. If you are dealing with cash, use some coupons or buy a generic brand and pocket any savings.

Try to sell some clothes to a consignment store. Then you can get cash back and stash it in a safe place, but start small, just a few dollars at a time. Find a safe place to put it. Try a shoe box that he would never look in or a pocket of an old jacket of *yours*. Hide it where he would not look, such as near the door, in the garage, under the children's bed, anywhere that you could grab it and run. Also pack and stash an extra set of clothes and some nonperishable food for yourself and your children.

Here are some other things to consider doing to prepare;

- Make a habit of backing the car into the driveway and keeping it fueled. Keep the driver's door unlocked and all the doors locked — for a quick escape.

- Get an extra set of keys made for the car and hide it with the cash – this could save you if he hides the keys.
- Make a getaway emergency plan. Know where you can go for at least one night.
- Keep any evidence of physical abuse, such as pictures and doctors reports if litigation is necessary.
- Don't leave without your driver's license
  - medications & medical records
  - credit cards or a list of credit cards you hold yourself or jointly (use page 72 to write these down)
  - checkbooks and information about bank   accounts and other assets
  - Pack this book to use as a reference!

If time is available, also take:

- ✓ Citizenship documents (such as your passport, green card, etc.
- ✓ Titles, deeds and other property information
- ✓ Children's school and immunization records.
- ✓ Insurance information

- ✓ Copy of marriage license, birth certificates, will and other legal documents
- ✓ Verification of social security numbers
- ✓ Welfare identification
- ✓ Valued pictures, jewelry or personal possessions

You may also create a false trail to throw him off if he is looking for you. Call motels, real estate agencies and schools in a town at least six hours away from where you plan to relocate in case he checks your phone records. Also, ask questions that require a call back to your house in order to leave phone numbers on record.

Write down phone numbers of family, friends, and your church. Above all, try to write down the information you need when you can't get the actual record to take with you, because then you will have that information here (see space below for such notes).

Don't forget this book!!

_____

_____

_____

_____

_____

_____

_____

_____

_____

_____

Tips for Escaping When There is Time to Plan

If you are lucky enough to have time to plan and family to lean on, then here are some suggestions for your escape. Everything from the above section applies. This section suggests some things for you to improve yourself while you prepare to getaway.

Most people who have been or are being abused have self esteem issues. Otherwise this wouldn't be happening to you.

Here are some other things to consider doing to prepare;

- Ask a friend or a family member to hold money for you. Be sure your abuser does not catch on.
- Create several believable reasons for leaving the house at different times of the day or night to introduce ways of getting out of the house.
- Call a domestic violence hotline occasionally to evaluate your options (e.g., room and board options) and get a supportive understanding ear.
  Remember: often, not always, the person on the end of the phone is a survivor as well.
  1.800.799. SAFE (7233)

- Keep a journal of all violent events, including the dates and the threats made. This could be helpful if you need to go to court to fight for custody of your child/children.
- Acquire job skills or take courses at a community college if you can.
    - If you are injured, go to a doctor or an emergency room and report what happened to you. Request that they document your visit. (ER's are now required to ask you if you feel safe at home.)
    - Have a phone nearby at all times. Consider hiding a prepaid cell phone to use in emergencies.
    - Create a code word with friends and family in order to communicate to them that you need help.

Safety with Technology

According to the National Domestic Violence Hotline http://www.ndvh.org/,

- Your computer activity can be monitored or checked without your knowledge. It is not possible to delete or clear all of the "footprints" from your computer or online activities. If you are being monitored, it may be dangerous to change your computer behaviors such as suddenly deleting your entire Internet history if that is not your regular habit.

- If you think you may be monitored on your home computer, be careful how you use your computer since an abuser might become suspicious. You may want to keep using the monitored computer for non-personal activities, like looking up the weather or reading the news. Use a safer computer (e.g., the local library or a friend's house) to research an escape plan, look for new jobs or apartments, bus tickets, or ask for help.

- Consider opening a free email account that your abuser doesn't know about. Only check it from public or otherwise safe computers (libraries, schools, and a friend's home).

- If you use have a cell phone, be aware that even calls that are toll-free will likely show up on your phone bill. If you are on a joint plan or access your phone bill online, others may have access. Consider making calls to shelters, lawyers, or other confidential services from a payphone or prepaid cell phone.

Call your local domestic violence program and ask them about free cell phone programs. Usually these phones will allow you dial 911.

Please call the 24-Hour National Domestic Violence Hotline at **1-800-799-SAFE (7233)** or TTY 1-800-787-3224 to discuss your concerns and questions.

Educate Yourself

Absorb yourself as much as possible with positive influences. It is necessary to learn to rethink. You need to learn to recognize a controlling personality to keep yourself from attracting the same kind of relationship. I used to say I was a bum magnet. I finally made an actual list of my requirements for a positive relationship and the traits they could and could not possess. My list was very specific. It required that a man must have a job (for at least three consecutive months), his own place to live and a life with hobbies of his own. When I made my list I was fed up from men coming in to my world, with less than I had, and just smelling up the place. After making my list I realized the type of men I consistently attracted were bums. It was partly my fault, because I didn't realize how unhealthy my choices were. My list opened my eyes to what my true priorities were/are. After visualizing my priorities on paper I found Rick, my wonderful husband. When I met him I was not looking for a relationship, because I was content with myself and my children. It seems I had to find that contentment before I could find peace in a relationship. I have never been happier. It is a very different feeling if you haven't been in a healthy relationship before. There really are good guys out there. Don't start looking, get out of your unhealthy relationship first, and then get started on the healing process of yourself. Learn to like being alone with you. It's a whole new world, which can be scary, but satisfying and liberating. Only then will you attract the right man.

I can remember waking up one night while we were camping and Rick was gone. The panic I felt from my past came rushing in; and then I realized he was probably at the restroom. Sure enough, he was back in a few minutes. I was so relieved to not have that fear anymore.

Pick up any book you can get your hands on about positive attitude, self help and how to find peace in your life. You will gain strength which will help you on your journey to free yourself from unhealthy relationship and the negative self destructive thought process. Plus, people are more attractive when they are self assured. Someone once asked me if I was afraid of being alone? They said It is better to be alone and lonely, than married and lonely.

Faith

Get to know your God, go to a church or just sit in your closet and talk to Him about whatever you want. He or She will listen. Trust me. He does not want you to live in danger or pain. When it was my time to finally leave, I told God I know this life is not what He had in mind for me or my children. I believe in the institution of marriage, so please don't be mad at me but please come with me, give me strength and help me to get out of here. You will be amazed at how things will fall into place once you ask for His help.

Where to Get Help

The National Domestic Violence Hotline

http://www.ndvh.org/get-help/safety-planning/#1

Hotline at **1-800-799-SAFE (7233**) or TTY

1-800-787-3224 to discuss your concerns and questions.

Ending abuse and violence in relationships is a community effort with plenty of people ready to help. Your local phone book will list crisis centers, help lines, and abuse hotlines. These organizations have professionally trained staff to listen, understand, and help. In addition, religious leaders, student health center, doctors, and other health professionals can be sources of support and information.

The intention for our stories is to reach you and change your life or the life of someone you know in a positive way.

Chapter 12

A Woman's Experience of the Physical Impact of

Stress from

Her Unhealthy Relationship

This is a true story of one young woman's struggle with serious illness symptoms, with the results being negative. You can make your own conclusions as you read her story.

I was a vibrant 30 something with two lively, adorable little kids, and a very self-centered alcoholic husband. I discovered I was a people pleaser. By doing everything for everyone else and forgetting my own health. I did my best to hold together the house, family and work full time. Our health is something we don't think about until it starts to diminish.

My life consisted of working 12-16 hour shifts, with little sleep, caring for my kids, with very little help from my husband. He added to my stress.

As a people pleaser, I strived to be the perfect wife. I did not nag, I rarely asked him to help with anything. I tried my best to keep a very clean home and make good, healthy meals, and, of course, make him happy in bed. Naturally, I internalized how much I hated his drinking. I gave 110% every single day to make up for how little he contributed to the family.

Every day as I drove home after working a 12 or 16 hour shift, the closer I got to home the tighter the knot in my stomach would get. My body would ache all over and this anguish was normal. Then my chest would hurt and I would get dizzy. The reason I felt this way, is that I would ask myself as I drove,

"What kind of mood will he be in tonight"? Is he going to yell at the kids for every little thing and virtually ignore me? I would hope that he would fall asleep early on the couch while I fed the kids, bathed them, cleaned the kitchen, did some laundry and prepared for the next day. I would still be working 3-4 hours after he had sat his drunken ass on the couch. I would cry at night, when everyone was asleep. This was my life.

It seemed like years since I'd even had a cold. Suddenly, I was frequently getting sick with serious ailments. My health was deteriorating at a rapid speed.

An infection began in my foot that turned into a summer long ordeal. After being in and out of the hospital and getting IV antibiotics, I was finally admitted for a week. That was horrible for me. My home fell apart during that time in so many ways. The first day I had to go to ER, my husband did not come to see me for hours and when he did he wore a pouty look that was evident that I was inconveniencing him; rather than a look of worry and concern that would be expected from the man who vowed to be at my side in sickness and in health. He fell asleep on my hospital bed. It would have been much nicer for him to show genuine concern for me and then go home out of compassion for me to get rest and to get better. Instead of the

"I'm here what more do you want from me." I was released from the hospital, even though I still had a fever of 102.

The fever of 102 persisted, I was not getting better. I felt I needed to go back to the hospital. My husband was too drunk to take me. In fact, he yelled at me about how nothing was wrong with me and that I shouldn't keep running to the hospital. Luckily, a friend was there and she took me. Again I went and came back with the results being negative, except for an unexplainable fever.

Days passed, and then finally, I became so weak I could barely walk or talk. My fever was still 102. I waited all night to return to the hospital again because of the impending tirade about him missing sleep. I finally woke him up and he didn't believe I needed to go. He made me call a nurse line to find out first and they said to take me immediately. He did, reluctantly. I was there for a week. The doctors were dumbfounded, and throwing out terms like meningitis and Methicillin-resistant Staphylococcus Aureus (**MRSA**) a bacterial infection that is highly resistant to some antibiotics. It is highly contagious and can be life threatening. After multitudes of test, the infectious Disease doctor announced that all results for infectious diseases were negative. The rash that was spreading all over my body and my heart racing were the cause of the combination of the three different antibiotics they were giving me. In other words, the medicines were actually making me sicker. So they took me off everything except a topical ointment for my foot.

Through all of this stress and worry, I had no comfort that my children were getting their basic needs met. I was even more anxious at the thought of my 4 and 6 year old being left with their, drunken father to take care of them.

I could not even take care of myself and I had to get better fast to be certain my children were being properly cared for. Slowly, I began to get better and finally went home.

A couple of weeks later, I started to get weak again., I had a horrible headache, my neck was stiff, and I developed a fever. The cycle continued throughout the entire summer months passed and the chest pain, dizziness and migraines were a daily occurrence. I started to worry more because what if I had something life threatening was wrong with me? I could not die and leave my children with their father, who was not willing to take care of them. My babies needed me.

I went to many doctor's appointments with many specialists and nothing was found. It got so bad that my chest hurt, I was dizzy and my hands tingled, and ended up in the ER again. I drove myself like I usually did. Even when I had a kidney stone, I drove myself. He never thought anything was wrong with me. They did expensive CT scans and sent me home. Why did I feel so horrible if nothing was wrong?

Thankfully, the supplements my naturopath suggested helped me get better within a few days. I believe Dr. Diana Alba; (www.pristinehealth.qwestoffice.net) has saved my live in many ways. She has taught me and my family to be responsible for our own health through diet and exercise in a natural way.

My mom and sister came to visit a couple weeks later. My mom did not get along with my husband (Hmm, I wonder why), and the tension in the house was unbearable. The house was full and I was doing my best to please everyone. (See a pattern here?)

While they were visiting, I went to bed, not feeling very well, but thought I could just sleep it off. In the middle of the night, I felt I should go to the bathroom. I developed this intense abdominal pain that was the worst pain I have ever felt. I had both my kids with no epidural and passed kidney stones un-medicated and this was still ten times worse pain. I sat there on the bathroom floor going through my head all the things that could be wrong with me. I have worked in the medical field for a long time, so I knew I was in deep trouble with abdominal pain this severe. My biggest fears were that my appendix burst or that my aorta ruptured. I knew I needed help but I was too weak to make any noise. The pain was so horrible that I could not move. I have never been so scared in my life. I thought I had to get help somehow or I could die right there. Again, I did not want my kids to be raised by their dad. I wanted to be with them. I had to find a way to get help, so I crawled back to the bedroom very slowly just thinking about my kids the entire way. The scary thing was I had to wake the sleeping, angry bear who hates to take me to the hospital. I made it to the bed and woke him. I still could not walk so he just dragged me down the stairs, yes dragged me, to the car. I wanted so much to kiss my kids goodbye but didn't want to wake them. I really thought I was going to die. There was nothing like that pain. He pulled up to the ER ambulance bay and the staff took me in by wheelchair. The lights swirled by and I just writhed and moaned in pain, hoping they could help me. They rushed me to get an abdominal Computed Tomography scan (CT), which uses X-rays and computers to produce images of a cross-section of the body. The patient must lie as still as possible as the table moves through the large, donut-shaped scanning device. Movement could blur the images produced by the scanner. Afterward they gave me IV pain meds. The pain began to subside and the doctor said my CT was negative. The appendix and aorta were ok.

I was so relieved and perplexed at the same time. How could I feel so horrible without a valid medical reason? What is wrong with me? As he drove me home, and he acted all grumpy because I ruined his night of sleep, I realized what was wrong. My life was making me sick. My mom said to me afterwards, you need to remove the stress from your life. What my mom meant was, I should cut back on activities and try not to do so much, and however, I knew what the true cause was. I continued to live that way for four more months.

We decided to go have a nice family dinner early on a Sunday evening. He actually looked up an online menu and told us all what we could order, to keep the cost down. I was disappointed that we could not all pick for ourselves what we wanted to eat. I like for the kids to get what they want, within reason, of course. He said to us on the drive over,

"Are you excited for dinner?"

I said, "I guess."

He looked at me with fire in his eyes and did not look or speak to me during the entire meal at the restaurant. I felt so bad for the kids. Daddy's mad again. We were in and out in less than an hour, in silence. The kids knew not to ask for anything.

This is our family time and it was like this every time we had "family time". He was always mad about something the kids or I did. At that moment, I realized I didn't want to live like that anymore. This is not good for me or the kids.

I spent the next few days planning to move and pulled a U-Haul truck up to the house exactly one week after our unpleasant family meal. That was the end of my health problems. I have a brand new life and have never been happier and healthier. I wish I had done something sooner but all that matters is I did something to finally take care of me and my children. It was evident that my man was bad for my health!

I have to say I am not without fault for my unsuccessful marriage. It takes two to make a good or bad relationship. I will say there is cause and effect, for example. His drinking caused me to be nervous and distrustful. My expectations of a marriage were one thing and his were another. I believed in a team atmosphere while his was of a dictatorship. I also learned it wasn't just his drinking but his selfishness that I could no longer tolerate.

I am taking time to get to know myself and understand my expectations for a relationship. I will be more particular in my next relationship. I will pay attention to how he treats his mother and how his father treats his wife, as those are his role models. Knowing now that I have tendencies to be a people pleaser, I have learned to keep a balance that includes taking care of me and my children. When I am ready to have another relationship I will be sure that my health and happiness are a priority.

Chapter 13

Psychological Endurance

Your mental state can save your life or it can kill you! Some will say "oh she must be very insecure to be in such a relationship" The truth is that "she" is a very strong person. You have to adapt to some very horrible situations to survive through them.

An example is in the following story written by a professional woman whom I recently met. She had originally asked that I not use her name. She later contacted me and realizing she is helping others, she said yes you can use my name; I am not ashamed it wasn't my fault.

She is an intelligent woman who survived a brutal attack, by remaining calm and controlled.

My friend shared her story with me after repressing it for over 20 years, all because, I was finally sharing my story.

A Story of Violent Rape and Healing

When I was 21, I moved to Denver to look for a job. I had graduated from the university and couldn't find a job in my hometown. I didn't have any friends or family there, other than a cousin I saw occasionally in a town several miles away. For about a year I worked as a Catering Manager in a restaurant. I was overworked: 20 hours a day, 6-7 days a week. I'd told my boss I was leaving – but would stay on long enough to hire and train my replacement.

Well, I did train my replacement. One evening my trainee said he wanted to take me to dinner, so I went with him. Afterwards he drove to his apartment before taking me home, saying that he had to get something. Once in the dark parking lot he asked me to come see some of his photographs. I said,

"No, just take me home." He pressured me three times. Finally I said,

"OK, but just for a minute, then I want to go home." Something inside me didn't want to go.

Once upstairs he started kissing me, but after a couple of minutes I said,

"I don't want to do this. Take me home now." Suddenly I saw something I'd never seen in anyone before – a rage and hate that sent chills throughout my body. I resisted with all my might, demanding that he stop and take me home! Instead he picked me up and carried me to the bedroom and threw me on the bed, landing on top of me. He was strangling me.

"If you scream or resist, you won't get away alive! I'm a brown belt in karate and know how to take you down."

He started ripping my clothes off. I was terrified. At that moment, I remembered a tattoo on my dad's arm from his war years, "Death before Dishonor." I felt that I wasn't ready to die, that I had more to do in the world. I just wanted to get out of there alive. Then I thought that maybe I could escape and run naked out to the common area and parking lot screaming for help, but he was a big, strong man and I couldn't even move.

Then I decided to use my mind, my intellect to get through this. He had one hand in a death grip around my neck and another on my inner thigh. I couldn't get away. Then he violently raped me; I thought I would die! I blocked out much of the rest, just praying to get out alive. Never before in my life had a man not listened to my simple request to stop, to not kiss me. I had no experience in this area.

Finally, after what seemed an eternity, it was over and he let me get up. I could not believe that he wanted me to spend the night! That's when I used my mind. I got up and casually went over to the bathroom, grabbing my clothes.

"Oh no thanks. I have to get some things done at home and get up early for work. Just take me home now."

I HAD to get out of there and home before he wanted to hurt me again. I closed the bathroom door and looked in the mirror. I was shaking so hard, my face was red and stained, my hair rumpled. But inside I was really quaking. An inner voice kept saying,

"Get out of here now!"

So I acted calm and controlled. I had him take me home. But when we got to my apartment parking lot he still asked me again to spend the night with him! I couldn't believe that he didn't understand that he had just raped me violently against my will! So I got out and said

"See you tomorrow."

Once inside the relative safety of my own apartment, I collapsed in a mess of tears and agony. I drew a warm bath and sat in the tub for what seemed like hours, dragging a wash cloth all over me to get rid of the stain, his filth. I felt so loathsome, dirty, disgusted, ravished, hurt, and physically sore. I hated myself, yet I knew that I had done nothing wrong, other than go out with a secret monster. I felt sure that he had done this to other women many times before. I kept remembering his eyes full of hate and rage. I wondered why he hated women so much; an ex-wife, a bad mother?

Finally, I got out of the bathtub and tried to get a little sleep, but could not. I had to see this man in a few short hours at work again. I was still terrified and couldn't stop shaking! In those days a woman didn't often tell the police about a rape. Those women who did were actually further victimized and accused of wanting it; they were shown on television and further traumatized. Those who went to trial were so rare they were televised on the local news. The rapist usually went free. Good grief, what further torture! Not for me, though I wished I had their courage to go forth and punish the rapist.

I don't remember much about the next day. I couldn't focus or concentrate. Inside I was shaking all the time. Later I told my boyfriend Nick. He was so sympathetic and helpful to me! Thank heavens! He was a black belt in karate and Chicago Street fighting.

He offered to go "take care of him for me!"

"Thanks," I said, "I really appreciate that, but I don't want anything to happen to you in case he files a police report. He's not worth it."

So instead he took me to a nearby Tae Kwon Do studio where he interviewed the Korean Master, Mister Ra. They spoke a few minutes and Nick, decided that this was a good place and he would be a worthy teacher for me. I started Tae Kwon Do at the very next class with about 20-30 other students of all ages. I went for an hour and a half three days a week. I liked my white uniform, patch and yellow belt. I loved the Kadas (special fight routines) and practicing all the different forms with legs and arms, but not so much the sparring.

I started with the intent of learning self-defense to better protect myself in case of future threats. But what I gained was much greater. I regained confidence, self-esteem, and belief in myself. I learned to say no and mean it and not take anything off of anybody.

But the nights alone were terrible. I slept with a camp knife under my pillow and with the light on all night. I had recurring nightmares, horrible flashbacks, and was hyper vigilant at all times. The slightest noise would start me trembling again. I could hardly eat. This went on for over a year!

I told my boss, but he wasn't very sympathetic, just said that's too bad, when really I thought he should have fired the guy and called the police! I did tell a couple of married male friends who were very caring and sympathetic; talking to them helped; I didn't feel so sleazy, but I still felt dirty, miserable. They said he was scum. I showed them the bruises across my neck and upper inner thigh. They were distinct purple blue big, long finger marks! They lasted for several weeks. My lips were bruised and swollen and my body ached all over. I needed my family. I needed their warmth and safety and love. I wanted to get away. I didn't want to tell my parents back home. My mother was dying of brain cancer and she and my dad had enough to worry about. I didn't want to add more misery to my sweet family. I wanted to support *them*. So I handled it pretty much alone. I told my boss I needed a couple of days off to get away and be with my family. It wasn't really a request, it was an

"I'm going no matter what." But he supported it. The long drive back to Texas in the sunshine and open road helped.

When the rapist asked me out again, at work no less, which I couldn't believe, I said,

"You've got to be kidding! You violated me against my will!"
He seemed surprised,

"I thought you wanted it." I said,

"What part of NO and kicking and screaming did you not understand?! You threatened MY LIFE! You left me with bruises. You said I wouldn't get out alive!"

He never really said he was sorry, but wanted to come to my apartment to talk. Against my better judgment I let him come over that night for a few minutes. We sat on the floor, because I had no furniture except a bed. After a few minutes of talking I made him leave and I shook like crazy afterwards, deciding that I would never let him in my apartment again. I don't remember what he said, but it didn't make me feel better.

The next day at work he sat in the manager's chair (even though I was training HIM) and started making derisive, insulting, sexual remarks to me, asking me out. He swatted me on my butt when I got a report off the desk. I'd had enough Tae Kwon Do and return of self-esteem by then to turn to him and say in a strong, commanding voice,

"DON'T YOU EVER DO THAT AGAIN!!!"

I glared at him and stormed out the door. I left within a few days. My boss never even told me thanks for doing such a great job all year.

I was proud of myself for being able to stand up to this rapist! He was really a weak man who preyed on unsuspecting women. He needed to be in prison. I realized that he was not really sorry or repentant of his evil actions. And he was a dangerous threat to other women. He later asked another young woman out (he was at least 8-10 years older than us). At least I warned her about him ahead of time and discouraged her from going out with him, but she did anyway. What was she thinking?

Anyway, this horrific event took me at least 10 years to get over! It sapped my inner strength, confidence, trust and I often felt afraid. I couldn't bear the awful nights, and asked my boyfriend if we could live together (so I'd feel safer). This was a new low for me to sink to the level of overriding my moral code of waiting until marriage to live together, another indication of how terrified and desperate I felt. Of course, living together had its benefits, but was for the wrong reasons, and it didn't work out.

Several months into a new job I told a girlfriend one night. She surprisingly minimized the agony I had gone through! Instead she said,

"Oh that's nothing. I loaned a boyfriend a lot of money one time and he never paid me back. I felt so violated." She kept on about this for quite a while. I told her I was sorry that he did this and that she felt so bad. But I hurt inside. I'd opened myself up to her and she had emotionally slapped me by not sympathizing. I vowed never to tell another woman or to trust her with a confidence again.

I took many self-defense courses through the years and taught many other women about personal safety and protection. I wanted to prevent anything so terrible from happening to them. No one deserves being treated like a piece of meat.

I always knew that this violent rape was not my fault, that it was HIS fault! However, I still felt dirty, shameful, and loathsome. It was a huge hit to my personal freedom and safety.

Today I would tell my daughter and others, Go out with a new man in a group of people. Never go to his apartment alone or have him to your place alone. Avoid using alcohol on dates. Get to know him in a social and work level at least a year or more before getting physically or emotionally involved. And to my daughter I would also say,

"You can always call me to come get you and protect you if something bad ever happens." DO report any rape to the police. Go to the hospital immediately for a sexual assault test (which in itself can be humiliating, but needed for proof). DO get good therapy right away and as often and for as long as is needed to help you get through the experience you probably won't ever forget."

Today I am a counselor, and a huge advocate of young women. Often they have been sexually assaulted, mostly in college, on dates and with alcohol involved. Because of date rape drugs they often have little to no memory of what happened. I also counsel women of all ages who have been raped. The damage to their self-esteem is terrible. It can lead to eating disorders, anxiety, and depression. It was in graduate school many years later I learned that for over a year I had suffered from PTSD – Post Traumatic Stress Disorder, an awful affliction. (I didn't even know to think about or be tested for the sexual diseases he could have transmitted to me!)

However, I had worked my way through it the best way I could – with prayer, Tae Kwon Do, a few supportive friends, and my family's natural optimism which was part of my makeup. The main thing that caused an internal shift in me after about a year of pain and suffering, though, was this – forgiveness. Not for me, for I had done nothing wrong, but for the despicable perpetrator, even though he was not contrite or sorrowful. That is not the whole goal of forgiveness. It's to release the fear and hate within, to be able to live a hopeful, productive life.

It was all up to me. I could choose to live in fear or to move ahead with courage. I decided that I didn't want to live the rest of my life in fear, with recurrent nightmares, and suffocating anxiety. Even decades later I remember sitting on the floor of my apartment praying,

"Heavenly Father, please protect me. Jesus set the example for forgiveness. You have told me that it is essential to love. I forgive this horrible man for all the awful things he did to me. I know that his actions will be punished in your time. So I forgive him. Please help me get through life happy and able to help others. I love you. In Jesus' name, Amen."

At that moment I felt a huge weight lifted out of my body. I felt freer, happier, and full of light. I knew I could go forward and be in charge of my own life. I wouldn't let this keep me down. And I began the next part of my life, having learned from the past and growing with new skills and inner strength.

Alice Baland
www.EatUpTheGoodLife.com

Chapter 14

Our Unscheduled Stop

This next story is added because I want you to see that my life has changed tremendously. I have gained confidence, self esteem, and I can wake up in the morning smiling and be grateful for all that I have lived through and all that I have. I am most grateful for my family and friends.

Because it's a really great story of adventure, excitement and terror it needed to be told.

If I can do it, so can you.

1973 Bellanca Citabria

My friend Connie and I began our adventure across the skies along with 15 other women, in five other airplanes, to Sun River Oregon. It was September 26, 2002, 7:00 am. The sun was just coming up on the horizon; the air was fresh, and crisp. We were the only ones at the airport that early. Our airplane was the slowest of the pack. In order to get to our destination close to the same time as everyone else we had to leave at least two hours before the others. There is a saying; "Time to spare, go by Air". It sure beats driving. We were flying a little two place tandem seated airplane called a 1973 Bellanca Citabria. It has a 150 horsepower Lycoming engine that holds 36 gallons of fuel and burns about eight gallons an hour. It cruised along at about 115 miles per hour. Because it was a slow airplane and didn't burn very much fuel, we were able to enjoy the scenery. Connie and I chatted along the way as the sun got higher in the sky. We looked forward to it being a beautiful day

The airplane was owned by a friend of ours. They were kind enough to allow me to fly it and we did the maintenance in return. It was a great deal for me, I just had to wash it and fly it. My husband, Rick did all the work. Fortunately, it was practically brand new so the only maintenance it required was the annual inspections. Rick was happy to do the maintenance. That way he knew it was a safe airplane and he was like a proud dad every time I took off. The plans for our trip included eating, drinking, shopping, and a little hiking and just general girl stuff. We rented two houses where we would share rooms with other gals. My passenger, and roommate for the weekend, was Connie. I loaded up the Citabria with our very small bags. There's not much room, and there are weight restrictions. We jetted off the ground after hugs and kisses from our loyal and supportive men. All was well as I checked the gauges, confirmed the fuel tanks were full; Rick filled it up for me the night before. We would be there in about two and a half to three hours and we have enough fuel for four hours. There should not be any winds that time of day that would cause us to be any slower.

Two and half hours passed by after we became airborne, and we were cruising along enjoying the beautiful morning with the calm winds and clear air. We were chatting away about normal family happenings. I was paying attention as we chatted, always looking at our direction and our altitude. I was feeling quite liberated that I was flying an airplane, with my friend, to a destination. It reminds me of the first time I was allowed to drive a car with a friend along.

Listening to the wonderful sound of the purring engine is such a calming sound. If it quits then that calm sound and security quickly becomes panic. When the engine stops it's always best to be your intentional decision, because you are landing. I occasionally looked at the ground to see where we could land if needed. It's beat into us when we become pilots to always be aware that if you had to land right now where you would go? And right then over miles of trees, with no where flat in sight, I was thinking

"Keep on going baby!!" I had it trimmed out, which means you have leveled the wings and adjusted the trim control so that the airplane will fly level without you having to have your hands on the controls at all times. So once in the air there is not much to do until we get close to our destination.

We came across the mountains just before the valley at Sun River. I began to let down from 8500 feet to Traffic Pattern Altitude (TPA) of 5100 feet. I like to be on top of things. When I glanced at the fuel gauges, I had to do a double take. I thought to myself

"What the heck! Why are they reading empty? It's only been two and a half hours; I should have another one and half hours left." They are a different type of gauge than what I was used to, and I had always been told to go by time, rather than the gauges. I was used to needle gauges in Cessna's. As long as the needle was bouncing I was ok. These gauges were not bouncing, in fact they are not moving at all. They actually said that I had no fuel. How could that be? What if the engine quits? Where the hell is Sun River? I was still 10 miles out. I was sure we would be OK but I was still nervous and sweating! My thoughts were racing. Where would we land? I remembered a round field a short ways back. I couldn't go back. I couldn't land in a round field- I needed a straight field. There was a very busy highway to the right of us and a huge band of trees in the center. On the left was a small frontage road with giant power lines crossing it. And then ... Out of nowhere the engine quits, Connie said,

"Do we have fuel?"

I look but don't answer. Oh my God, what do I tell her? I was doing my best to remain calm and give her something to do so she wouldn't start screaming,

"Were going to die!"

I just said

"look for the airport. I can't see it."

I kept my thoughts to myself, hoping not to scare Connie. Who was going to keep me calm?

"Oh my God! What is happening? I pushed in mixture to be sure it wasn't being starved for fuel. Thank God, the engine started! Climb, climb, climb; we need altitude! Why did I let down when we are still 10 miles out? We gained about 500 feet. Whew! That was scary, and what if it happens again?

"No it can't. I can't do this, I'm not skilled enough."

"Crap! It quit again! I push and turn anything and everything and it goes again. I'm scared! Where can we land?"

"I see a railroad track… nope,…OK what are my options?"

My other option is the small road lined with high tension wires and very tall trees. If I go there, we could be killed; but if I go on the highway, we will definitely take someone else out with us.

There it was again… silence.

"Oh my God! This can't be happening! We are going down, whether we want to or not!"

My thought processes were very scattered and panicky. I was shaking, and I really wanted to cry and let someone else take over; but I can't cry. I can't give up! I have to fly this airplane to the best of my ability. I have to do this or we are going to die. Not just die, we could burn. I told myself to focus on my training. Focus. Remember the emergency procedures you just did 3 days ago. Find your spot and land the airplane. You can do this. Don't look at the power lines.

"It's just an airplane, and another airport," I thought, trying to convince myself.

I noticed Connie is rubbing my shoulders and telling me

"You can do it, you can do it."

Thank God she's calm I couldn't take it if she had been freaking out. She calmed me down.

"Okay," I thought, "We can do this."

It's time to let someone know what's happening, to let some know where we are, so they can send fire trucks and get here quickly to cut us out, if necessary. Just then a Citation was entering the area. The pilot had just turned to the frequency in time to hear my very high pitched voice say,

"This is Citabria 008, I'm declaring an emergency,"

A calm, and a little annoyed voice said,

"Where are you?" I'm sure the pilot thought, some girl was freaking out and it was going to delay their landing.

Frantically, and barely able to breath, I answered,

"I'm eight miles from Sun River. I have no other options, and I have no oil pressure." (That's what I found out later that I said, it sounded better than, admitting I had no fuel.). As we turned to make a final approach I thought

"This is going to be bad! God help us!" I also heard

"Focus, fly the airplane. You can do it." If the wings rip off, stay focused. Don't stop flying the airplane. Focus, focus, focus! "

We were descending, but we were too high to get under the high tension wires. I had to slip (angle the airplane with the left wing down to the side so it speeds the descent, but doesn't move the airplane forward any faster, instead of straight and level. It's the only way to get under the power line.

IF WE TOUCH IT WE'LL BE ELECTROCUTED! I thought

"It's working Oh my God we cleared it. Wait! We're not done yet. I hurried to flip it to the right to get around the curve of the road. Don't let the airplane touch down yet! Hold it off the ground, OK, straighten out. Get the wings level and quickly!"

"There's a car on the road!"

"Get out of the way!"

"Please move!"

"Hurry"

The car swerved off the road safely. Then finally, chirp, chirp, the sound of the tires just barley touching the ground and rolling out.

"We made it, oh my god we made it," my heart was beating out of my chest.

Now that we were on the ground there was new danger. Since we were in the middle of the road, just beyond a blind curve that was the best landing I ever made. I was afraid cars would come around the coming around the corner and hit us.

I yelled "Hurry, Connie! Get out! Hurry!"

The Citations pilot's voice raised a little as he realized this was serious,

The Pilot asks

"Where are you now?"

I told him, "52478 Huntington Road".

"Is that a mile marker?" he asked

"No, it's an address, we are on a road."

"We're down we are OK." I heard him tell someone

"She's on a road, and she's OK!

Once we were safely out of the airplane, I immediately called my husband. I really needed to hear his voice. He answered the phone saying,

"Oh you are there already?" I explained,

"Well not really, I had to land on a road because I ran out of fuel." All he could say was,

"You ran out of fuel! You ran out of fuel!" I could hear the fear and a little anger in his voice.

"Do you know how many places you passed?" He knew I was alright because I was talking to him, then all he wanted to know was,

"Why did you run out of fuel?"

"You should have had plenty, what's wrong with the airplane?"

"Do you see any fuel stains on the wings or stabilizer?" I assured him that there were none. He continued questioning me.

"Is anything dripping from the carburetor?" I told him that it was completely dry. He could not figure it out based on what I explained. I did not have time to figure it out because the police and fire trucks were coming, so I told him that I would call him back. I wondered out loud whether they would let me fly out from the highway. Rick said he would fly up and get me out, but I assured him that I could do it.

"Oh my God I can be up there in a couple hours." Now was really worried.

"No," I said

"I think I can fly it out of here. I'll call you back."
He said,

"Make sure, you really make sure! I wish I was

there, call me back. Please be careful. I love you."

The police arrived and were very nice and
helpful;

I said, "I think I can fly it out of here," thinking
they were going to laugh at me and say,

"Hell no little lady!" Instead it turns out the main
police officer is a pilot! He said,

"Wow! You did a great job getting it in here!"
"How about you taxi down the road here to the State
Highway 97 and we will block it off for you." "There are
no wires, and the road is much wider." I told him

"I was up for it, but that I would need fuel."

The police confirmed that they would radio to
the airport and ask them bring some fuel out to me."

By now the media had arrived as well as the other ladies we were meeting had heard about our adventure. They all jumped into their cars and drove to the scene. My plan was to have them drive Connie and our bags to the airport. I wanted to be as light as possible when I took off from the road. If anything else happened it would only happen to me, and not Connie. We pushed the aircraft over to the side of the road with just the wing still out in the road. Only one car at a time could pass. A large Dodge truck with three guys pulled up and said

"How'd you get that in here?"

Connie told them, "Oh we just had an unscheduled stop." Just then a guy in the back rolls down his window and said,

"You wanna see our Bear?" Then Connie looked in the back of the truck to see a huge brown bear that had been killed! She yelled to me as I was on the phone with Rick,

"They have a bear in the truck!"

"What? That's crazy!" Sure enough it was bear hunting season.

The very nice men from the airport brought out ten gallons of fuel and I was ready to go. First though, one of the firemen came to look inside the aircraft said, "Just wanted to see what it looks like in here in case I have to cut you out." Sarcastically, I said

"Oh thanks, I feel better now."

The police officer drove me down the road where I was going to take off so I could scope it out. We agreed that he would stand down the road, still in my view and tell me if the aircraft was smoking and give me thumbs up if all was well. So they blocked the highway and I very calmly taxied down to the intersection. About 30 spectators had gathered. Somehow I was calm. I kept hearing Rick's voice, always telling me to pay attention to what I am doing and fly the airplane, rather than worrying about how your hair looks. So I pushed in the throttle and the officer gave me the thumbs up. After I maneuvered around the street signs, I was ready to take off. As I lifted off I looked down over the line of cars being held at the end of the road. Cars were backed up for a mile! I told them I was sorry for their delay, but they didn't hear me...of course.

The Citabria has a limited instrument panel and only the necessary gauges. They all appeared to be working correctly. I radioed Sun River and made my approach. I landed, and everything was good. No one was there. I had a moment to myself. I was shaking a little. No time to break down. I'd do that later. I still had work to do. I needed to call Rick, tie down the airplane, and get it filled with fuel.

The Citation pilots showed up and said, "I just

want to shake your hand and congratulate you for doing a great job." That was pretty cool.

The next morning I flew the Citabria around to get back on the horse. I was very nervous. However, it was important to determine the amount of fuel that the airplane was using. We were scheduled to head back home in a couple of days and I needed to be sure the airplane was in working order. I didn't want to experience the road landing again. We were very fortunate with that outcome. Right now my luck was good. I really didn't want to push it. At this point I was still extremely nervous. My stomach had a huge knot in it and my hands were sweating. We really didn't know why the airplane ran out of fuel, and it could happen again. By my calculations the amount of fuel used on my test flight appeared to be normal.

Later we found out that the fuel cap wasn't completely tight. As a result the fuel was being siphoned out during the entire flight. I could not see this since it was a high winged airplane and the fuel fill spout was on top of the wing, not in my view.

It was an extremely scary experience but I learned that I can do anything that I put my mind to it, and you can to.

In the photo, Connie and I are talking to a Police officer. Notice the power lines and that we are stopped just past the curve.

Pilot out of gas lands plane on Huntington Road

by Cari Lampshire, New Berry Eagle and Barney Lorien, bend.com

A power plane was sputtering plane through power lines to make an emergency landing on Huntington Rd. south of Sunriver Sept. 26.

Sunny Adkins told arriving deputies that she and a friend, Connie Jackson, were on their way from Prairieville, Calif. to Sunriver Resort when his 1973 single-engine Bellanca Citabria plane ran out of fuel, forcing her to set down, swooping around the power lines along the road.

"It was really scary," she recalled, "and I was thankful I can take a vehicle course on emergency procedures."

Adkins landed nearby

Highway 97 because of the heavier traffic. Even on Huntington, she said several cars were heading right for her as she came in, but the motorists acted fast and pulled over.

"She did a great job – avoided the power lines, no new harm," said sheriff's Lt. Mike Johnson.

Aviation fuel was brought to the location, and roads in the immediate area were shut down so Adkins could take off and complete her flight to Sunriver. The incident was

Huntington Road became an emergency landing strip for Sunny Adkins when her plane ran out of gas while enroute to Sunriver Airport.

forwarded to the Federal Aviation Administration

Adkins – whom husband is a plane mechanic – said she should have gotten fuel before

of flying, come from the load of fuel, and only had been flying for three hours when the engine started sputtering. She tried to increase altitude to get more glide capability – her in so doing when little fuel was left drained out of the carburetor and basically "starved the engine," Adkins said.

Jackson, her passenger, said, "I wasn't concerned. I've flown with her before. She did a great job – she was shocking and diving and going under those power lines!"

This is the Highway they blocked off,
Making it safe for me to take off.

Resources

Great Books to Read

<u>The Erroneous zones</u>. Wayne Dyers

<u>Happy for no Reason</u> by Marci Shimoff

<u>10-10-10</u> by Suzy Welch<u>Finding your way</u>

<u>through Domestic Violence</u>

 By Constance Fourre`

<u>You Don't have to take it anymore</u> By Steven

Stosny PhD

<u>Cash in a Flash</u> by Mark Victor Hansen and

Robert G. Allen

<u>A woman's guide to balancing life in today's fast</u>

<u>paced world</u> by Caroline A. Wadlin, MD

Giving Back

Because I truly believe in the inspiration and support provided by the National Domestic Violence Hotline, I am donating a percentage of the proceeds generated from this book to their organization.

The National Domestic Violence Hotline receives 22, 000 calls a month. Millions have made changes in their lives because of the kindness and commitment of caring advocates on the other end of the phone. They have 15 years of dedication to changing the way America thinks about the once silent killer, Domestic Violence.

The National Domestic Violence Hotline has assisted in changing laws throughout the country. They also know their work is not finished. Their many advocates tirelessly fight for new laws to assist women to safety.

The many caring advocates and counselors are standing by to assist with expert advice and words of kindness and understanding.

The National Domestic Violence Hotline is **1.800.799. SAFE (7233)** and they are dedicated to your safety and standing by waiting for your call. This is an invaluable tool. Share it with your friends.

Go to http://www.ndvh.org/get-help/help-in-your-area/ to find help in your area.

1.800.799. SAFE (7233) 1.800.787.3224 **(TTY)**

Their help is Anonymous & Confidential 24/7

www.ingramcontent.com/pod-product-compliance
Lightning Source LLC
Chambersburg PA
CBHW072200090426
42740CB00012B/2332